# WHAT ARE CARBOHYDRATES?

DANIEL E. HARMON

Britannica®
Educational Publishing

IN ASSOCIATION WITH

ROSEN
EDUCATIONAL SERVICES

Published in 2019 by Britannica Educational Publishing (a trademark of Encyclopædia Britannica, Inc.) in association with The Rosen Publishing Group, Inc.
29 East 21st Street, New York, NY 10010

Distributed exclusively by Rosen Publishing.
To see additional Britannica Educational Publishing titles, go to rosenpublishing.com.

First Edition

**Britannica Educational Publishing**
J.E. Luebering: Executive Director, Core Editorial
Mary Rose McCudden: Editor, Britannica Student Encyclopedia

**Rosen Publishing**
Kathy Kuhtz Campbell: Senior Editor
Nelson Sá: Art Director
Nicole Russo-Duca: Series Designer and Book Layout
Cindy Reiman: Photography Manager
Nicole DiMella: Photo Researcher

**Library of Congress Cataloging-in-Publication Data**

Names: Harmon, Daniel E., author.
Title: What are carbohydrates? / Daniel E. Harmon.
Description: New York, NY: Britannica Educational Publishing in Association with Rosen Educational Services, 2019. | Series: Let's find out! good health | Audience: Grades 1–4. | Includes bibliographical references and index.
Identifiers: LCCN 2017045761 | ISBN 9781538302903 (library bound) | ISBN 9781538302910 (pbk.) | ISBN 9781538302927 (6 pack)
Subjects: LCSH: Carbohydrates—Juvenile literature. | Carbohydrates in human Nutrition—Juvenile literature.
Classification: LCC QP701 .H3545 2017 | DDC 613.2/83—dc23
LC record available at https://lccn.loc.gov/2017045761

Manufactured in the United States of America

# CONTENTS

# What Are Carbohydrates?

The body gets fuel from chemicals and other substances that provide energy. Carbohydrates—"carbs," as people sometimes call them—are the main sources of energy for most people. Sugar, starch, and cellulose are important forms of carbohydrates.

There are different kinds of sugar. The body needs certain types of natural sugar in regular amounts. Fruit, honey, and milk contain natural sugars. Other types of sugar are made by processing methods. Processed sugars are not necessary for human health. They are used largely as sweeteners for other types of food.

Raisins, prunes, apricots, and dates are examples of foods that contain natural sugar.

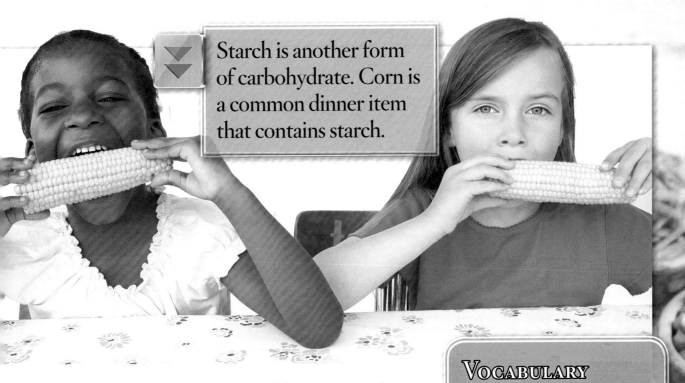

Starch is another form of carbohydrate. Corn is a common dinner item that contains starch.

Starch is produced by green plants. Corn, wheat, rice, and other grains contain starch. So do such vegetables as potatoes and beans.

Cellulose is a type of fiber contained in plants. Humans cannot digest dietary fiber, but fiber is important because it keeps the digestive system active.

Whatever sources they come from, carbohydrates are vital for human health. But it is important for people to understand the sources and to favor "good" carbs over "bad" carbs.

# How Carbohydrates Are Created

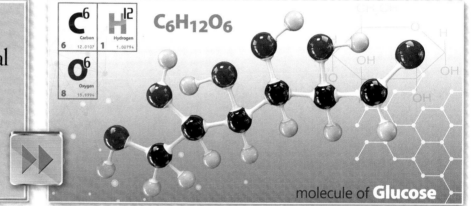

This is a scientific model of a chemical compound called glucose. Glucose is a type of carbohydrate.

$C_6H_{12}O_6$

| C[6] Carbon 6 12.0107 | H[12] Hydrogen 1 1.00794 |
| O[6] Oxygen 8 15.9994 | |

molecule of **Glucose**

The word "carbohydrate" is formed from the words "carbon" and "hydrogen." That is because carbohydrates are combinations of the chemical elements carbon and hydrogen, plus oxygen. The process of combining elements produces what scientists call a chemical compound. In the natural world, carbohydrates are the most common chemical compounds used for food.

Sunlight enters plants through their leaves. Plants convert sunlight into energy and store it in their fruit, which animals consume.

## Think About It

Why do scientists call carbohydrates "naturally occurring" chemical compounds?

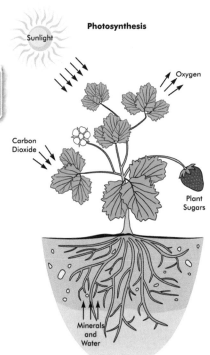

A process called photosynthesis produces carbohydrates and other compounds. In photosynthesis, plants convert energy from sunlight into chemical energy. Plants store this energy in the form of carbohydrates. Humans and other animals that eat plants take in these carbohydrates as nutrients that are necessary for growth and good health.

Photosynthesis is an example of why the sun is so important for life on Earth. It is much more than a source of natural heat and light. It also interacts with plant life to provide nourishing food for humans.

# Why Carbs Are Important

Carbohydrates are not only one of the body's major nutrients. They are the most common and healthiest source of energy. Carbohydrates in breakfast foods help to keep children alert and active at school.

Dieticians suggest that most of the calories people consume should be in the form of carbohydrates. A calorie is a measure of energy. Different foods contain different levels of calories.

This nutrition facts label shows the number of calories and the amount of carbs and other nutrients in the food.

| Nutrition Facts | |
|---|---|
| 8 servings per container | |
| **Serving size** | **2/3 cup (55g)** |

| Amount per serving | |
|---|---|
| **Calories** | **230** |

| | % Daily Value* |
|---|---|
| **Total Fat** 8g | **10%** |
| Saturated Fat 1g | **5%** |
| *Trans* Fat 0g | |
| **Cholesterol** 0mg | **0%** |
| **Sodium** 160mg | **7%** |
| **Total Carbohydrate** 37g | **13%** |
| Dietary Fiber 4g | **14%** |
| Total Sugars 12g | |
| Includes 10g Added Sugars | **20%** |
| **Protein** 3g | |
| Vitamin D 2mcg | 10% |
| Calcium 260mg | 20% |
| Iron 8mg | 45% |
| Potassium 235mg | 6% |

\* The % Daily Value (DV) tells you how much a nutrient in a serving of food contributes to a daily diet. 2,000 calories a day is used for general nutrition advice.

## COMPARE AND CONTRAST

Some people believe carbohydrates are a dangerous source of calories, resulting in weight problems. What is the difference between carbs and calories? How are carbs and calories related?

Besides carbohydrates, proteins and fats are major sources of calories. All three calorie sources are necessary for good health.

In addition to providing the body's energy supply, carbohydrates are an important source of dietary fiber. Fiber helps people to digest their food. Scientists also think that fiber helps to prevent heart disease, certain types of cancer, and diabetes mellitus (one of the two types of diabetes).

A boy gets fiber by eating an apple. The apple's skin is an especially good source of fiber.

# Simple and Complex Carbohydrates

Simple carbohydrates are the basic type of carbs. Soft drinks, candy, cookies, and other sweet snacks contain simple carbohydrates. These foods are often made with white sugar, a form of processed sugar.

Simple carbohydrates also are found in natural sugars. Fruit, milk, and vegetables contain natural sugars. Honey is a natural sugar as well. People eat natural sugar in its original form.

These are examples of foods containing simple carbohydrates. Many simple carbs are in processed sugar.

To produce processed sugar, food manufacturers make changes to natural sugars.

Complex carbohydrates are combinations of simple carbohydrates. Complex carbs are found in certain vegetables and grains. Starchy foods such as bread, rice, and potatoes are rich in complex carbs. Fiber also is a complex carbohydrate. Unprocessed foods such as whole grains contain more fiber than processed foods.

## THINK ABOUT IT

Simple carbs include the kind of sugar found in candy as well as sugars that are contained in vegetables and fruits—natural sugars. Why do you suppose natural sugars are better for a person's health?

Sweet potatoes are among the foods that contain complex carbohydrates.

# THREE CATEGORIES OF CARBOHYDRATES

The body uses three main categories of carbohydrates. They are monosaccharides, disaccharides, and polysaccharides. The term "saccharide" means "sugar."

A monosaccharide is made up of a single molecule of sugar. A molecule is the tiniest part of a substance that has all the characteristics of the substance. A monosaccharide is called a simple sugar. Fructose, a type of natural sugar contained in fruits, is a monosaccharide. Other monosaccharides are glucose and galactose.

Watermelon contains fructose, a form of natural sugar called a monosaccharide.

Sucrose is also known as table sugar. It often is used in baking. Sucrose is a type of disaccharide.

Two monosaccharide molecules joined together form a disaccharide. Sucrose and lactose are types of sugar in the disaccharide category.

A polysaccharide is made up of many monosaccharides. It may consist of a few monosaccharides or as many as ten thousand. Starches and fibers are polysaccharides.

Only simple sugars can enter the bloodstream and travel through the body. Monosaccharides are simple sugars, so they can enter the blood without being broken down. Disaccharides and polysaccharides are broken down into simple sugars during digestion.

**THINK ABOUT IT**

Why do you think carbohydrates must be broken down into smaller units before they can enter the bloodstream?

# CARBOHYDRATES AND DIGESTION

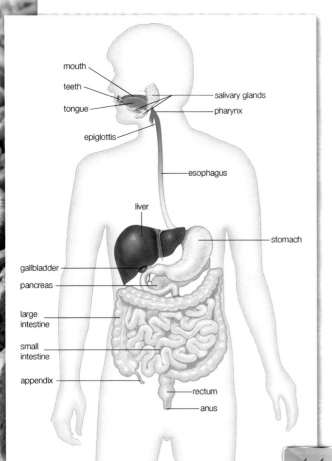

- mouth
- teeth
- tongue
- salivary glands
- pharynx
- epiglottis
- esophagus
- liver
- stomach
- gallbladder
- pancreas
- large intestine
- small intestine
- appendix
- rectum
- anus

Before carbohydrates in food can enter the bloodstream and provide energy for the body, they must be broken down into usable particles. This process occurs in the digestive system.

It takes thirty to forty hours for a complete meal to pass through the digestive system, from the mouth through the intestines. Most of the breaking-down process takes place in the stomach and small intestine.

The organs of the digestive system break down nutrients so they can enter the bloodstream and provide energy.

A calorie-counter app on a smartphone shows how many calories and carbs are contained in a banana. People with diabetes need to keep track of the carbs they consume.

During digestion, complex carbohydrates are divided into simple sugars. Chemicals called enzymes perform this process. Enzymes break starches and larger sugars into simple sugars such as glucose, fructose, and galactose. These

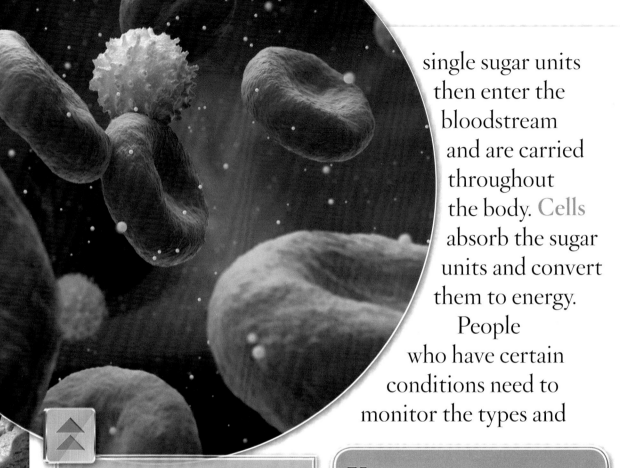

single sugar units then enter the bloodstream and are carried throughout the body. Cells absorb the sugar units and convert them to energy. People who have certain conditions need to monitor the types and

This illustration shows tiny units of glucose, a simple sugar, flowing through the bloodstream. The larger shapes are red and white blood cells.

## Vocabulary

**Cells** are the smallest units with the basic properties of life. Human beings are made up of more than seventy-five trillion cells.

# Glycemic Index

A glycemic index chart shows which foods may raise blood sugar levels more quickly than others.

| | |
|---|---|
| • white wheat bread, donuts, baguette, crackers, waffles<br>• white rice, boiled potatoes and mash, french fries<br>• watermelon<br>• cornflakes | **70 - 100** |
| • rye & wholegrain bread<br>• muesli, corn, couscous, brown rice, spaghetti, popcorn, yams<br>• ice cream, sweet yogurt<br>• banana, grapes, kiwi | **50 - 70** |
| • coarse barley bread<br>• strawberries, apples, pears, oranges<br>• milk & soy milk<br>• natural yogurt<br>• oatmeal, beans | **30 - 50** |
| • pearled barley, lentils<br>• grapefruit, cherry, apricot, plum<br>• dark chocolate 70% cocoa<br>• whole milk<br>• cashews, walnuts | **10 - 30** |
| • hummus, chickpeas<br>• garlic, onion, green pepper<br>• eggplant, broccoli, cabbage, tomatoes<br>• mushrooms<br>• lettuce | **0 - 10** |

### COMPARE AND CONTRAST

Which would raise a person's blood sugar faster—a piece of candy or a salad? Which is made of simple carbs and which has complex carbs?

amounts of carbohydrates that they digest. Many people perform a daily meal planning exercise called carb counting. They also may use a measurement called the glycemic index (GI). Foods with a high GI can raise blood sugar levels more quickly.

# Healthy Carbs for Children

Because carbohydrates are the body's main energy source, they are especially vital to growing, active children. Parents must make sure their children receive a proper portion of "healthy" carbs. Healthy carbs are rich in nutrients, not just simple sugars.

Dieticians urge people to consume most of their carbohydrates in natural forms. These include the starches in whole grains, nuts, seeds, legumes, and vegetables. They also include the sugars in milk, fruit, and other naturally sweet plant foods.

This dish of whole wheat pasta and green vegetables provides necessary carbohydrates and is light in calories.

The amount of exercise people get helps to determine how many calories they need. At least half of calories consumed should be carbohydrates.

Health professionals recommend that at least half of the calories in a typical diet come from carbohydrates. Boys and girls who are seven or eight years old and moderately active need about 1,600 calories each day. If they are very active, they need 200 to 400 more calories. That means that children should consume at least 800 calories of carbohydrates each day.

**THINK ABOUT IT**

Why do you think dieticians want people to consume most of their carbohydrates in natural forms?

# Low-Carb Diets

Many people believe that diets low in carbohydrates and high in proteins are the best way to lose weight. Although both carbs and proteins contain calories, these people think sugar and other carbohydrates cause weight gain. They argue that proteins help to build muscles and strengthen the body against disease. It seems to make sense.

A meal of salmon and vegetables provides a good supply of protein. Fish, meat, dairy products, and beans are all sources of protein.

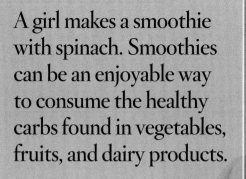

A girl makes a smoothie with spinach. Smoothies can be an enjoyable way to consume the healthy carbs found in vegetables, fruits, and dairy products.

However, dieticians warn that juggling carbohydrates and proteins in a diet can be risky. One reason is that low-carb diets may not provide enough vitamins for the body. A shortage of one vitamin, folic acid, increases the danger of strokes, heart disease, and hypertension. If a pregnant woman does not take in enough folic acid during pregnancy, her baby's spine and brain may not develop normally. At the same time, diets that are high in protein can be harmful to people who have kidney diseases or other health problems.

# "Loading" Carbohydrates

While some people turn to low-carb diets to lose weight, many athletes load up on carbohydrates. Their trainers may recommend at least 3 grams (0.1 ounce) of carbohydrates per day for every kilogram (35.3 oz.) that they weigh.

Some athletes take carb loading to an extreme. They consume as many as 12 grams (0.4 oz.) of carbs daily for each kilogram of body weight. That means that an athlete who weighs 80 kilograms (175 pounds) would take in between 240 and 960 grams (between

A student serves pasta before the Boston Marathon. Many athletes load up with carbs before competing.

Professional cyclists need plenty of carbs. They rely on carbs for energy during lengthy events.

8.5 and 33.9 oz.) of carbohydrates every day.

The main reason for loading up with carbs is to provide fuel for the muscles that athletes want to strengthen. During digestion, the body breaks down carbohydrates into glucose, a simple sugar. An athlete's muscles burn a lot of this sugar quickly. But the body stores some carbs temporarily, so they can supply energy later. Stored carbs do not make athletes stronger, but they help athletes to have the energy to exercise longer. In general, a generous amount of healthy carbohydrates in the diet is good for everyone's physical fitness.

COMPARE AND CONTRAST

Do you think carb loading is a good idea for everyone or just for athletes?

# Problems Caused by Carbs

Too much of a good thing can be bad. This old saying is true of carbohydrates. Even though they are necessary for good health, too many of them can lead to obesity, cardiovascular disease, or other health problems.

## Vocabulary

Cardiovascular disease is an illness of the heart and the vessels that circulate blood throughout the body.

French fries are not an ideal source of carbohydrates. Eating too many carbs can lead to ill health.

Diabetes mellitus is a dangerous disease related to sugar. It is estimated that more than four hundred million people around the world have a form of diabetes. A person with diabetes has difficulty processing glucose, a simple sugar that results from digesting carbohydrates.

People at risk for developing diabetes can take steps to prevent it. These steps include losing weight and limiting the sugary carbohydrates that they eat. If diabetes develops and is not treated, the results can be disastrous. The kidneys, legs and feet, and fingers can be damaged. The person can become blind. Diabetes also increases the danger of strokes and heart diseases.

# CARBOHYDRATES AND DENTAL HEALTH

Tooth decay is a common health problem linked to an excess of the wrong kinds of carbohydrates in a person's diet. Both natural and processed sugars can contribute to the formation of cavities.

Bacteria that collects in the mouth mingles with sugar and starch to create acids. These acids gradually eat away the enamel that shields teeth. Cavities result.

The risk of tooth decay is greater for people who eat sugary snacks between meals. The risk also increases when people eat sweets that dissolve slowly in the mouth.

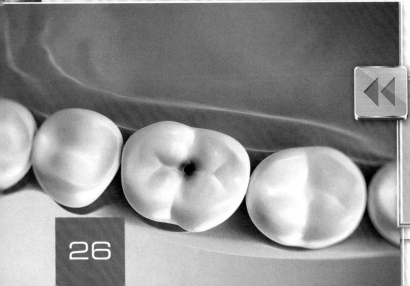

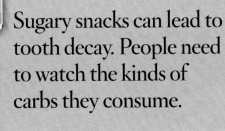

Sugary snacks can lead to tooth decay. People need to watch the kinds of carbs they consume.

A dentist checks for cavities and other signs of tooth problems. Problems can worsen if not detected early during regular checkups.

While carbohydrates can be linked to dental problems, so can other factors. For some people, tooth problems are hereditary. Certain medicines can affect oral health. Most important, if a person neglects daily dental hygiene and regular dental checkups, problems will arise sooner or later.

## THINK ABOUT IT

Do you think carbohydrates are the main cause of tooth problems for members of your family?

# MANAGING CARBS

A student with a headache tries to focus during class. Headaches can result from an imbalance of carbohydrates in the diet.

Most people understand that carbohydrates are among the most important nutrients. Many people, though, find it hard to maintain the right balance of carbs in their diets. Some consume too few carbohydrates. This situation increases their risk of developing certain health problems. Others consume too many carbs, or they eat lots of foods with high levels of less nutritious carbs. This situation, too, can result in medical problems.

**THINK ABOUT IT**

Nutritionists tell people to use common sense when choosing foods. What is a commonsense way to choose carbohydrates?

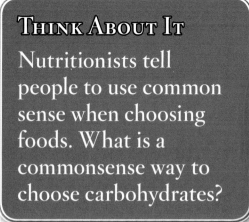

Porridge is a meal of boiled grain, such as oatmeal. It contains a high amount of healthy carbohydrates.

Health scientists explain that most people should not focus on cutting out or loading up on carbs. Instead, people should learn to manage their intake of carbohydrates. They should understand which forms of sugar and starch are most nutritious. They need to know which foods contain "smart carbs," such as unprocessed foods and foods rich in fiber.

In the end, a good diet plan includes healthy amounts of different types of carbohydrates. By learning about nutrition, young people can begin making wise eating choices at an early age.

# Glossary

**cavity** A hole formed in a tooth by decay.

**chemical element** A basic substance that cannot be broken down into simpler substances; a building block of all matter.

**dietary** Relating to a diet or the rules of a diet.

**enamel** A hard outer layer that covers the crown of a tooth.

**folic acid** A vitamin needed to produce red blood cells.

**hereditary** Passed from a parent to children.

**hygiene** Practices such as cleanliness that help a person stay healthy.

**hypertension** High blood pressure.

**intestine** A long tube, made up of small and large sections, in the digestive tract between the stomach and anus.

**legume** A plant food that grows in a pod—for example, beans, lentils, peas, and peanuts.

**macronutrient** A food substance needed in large amounts to maintain health.

**nutrient** A food substance or ingredient that provides nutrition for the body.

**obesity** The condition of having a large amount of body fat.

**oral** Near or related to the mouth.

**organism** A living person, plant, or animal.

**processed** Changed by special treatment, such as adding or removing ingredients, before being packaged and sold.

**stroke** A sudden weakening or loss of consciousness caused by the blocking of a blood vessel to the brain.

**whole grains** Grains, also called cereals, that contain all the natural nutrients of the entire grain seed.

# For More Information

## Books

*Are You What You Eat? A Guide to What's on Your Plate and Why!* New York, NY: DK Publishing, 2015.

Bailey, Megan. *Healthy Eating Choices.* Mankato, MN: Child's World, 2014.

Dickmann, Nancy. *What You Need to Know About Obesity* (Fact Finders). North Mankato, MN: Capstone Press, 2016.

Ivanoff, George. *Carbohydrates* (What's in My Food?). Mankato, MN: Smart Apple Media, 2012.

Lin, Grace, Ranida T. McKneally, and Grace Zong. *Our Food: A Healthy Serving of Science and Poems.* Watertown, MA: Charlesbridge, 2016.

Pelkki, Jane Sieving. *Healthy Eating* (A True Book). New York, NY: Children's Press/Scholastic Inc., 2017.

Ventura, Marne. *12 Tips for a Healthy Diet* (Healthy Living). Mankato, MN: 12-Story Library, 2017.

## Websites

**Choose My Plate**
https://www.choosemyplate.gov
Facebook and Twitter: @MyPlate

**GETFITTN**
https://www.getfit.tn.gov/kids/food-myths.aspx

**KidsHealth**
http://kidshealth.org/en/kids/carb.html
Twitter: @KidsHealth

# Index